Celebrating the Mass

Confronting the Brokenness of the World

Gerald Darring

www.Lulu.com
Lulu Enterprises, Inc.

Celebrating the Mass
by Gerald Darring

Copyright © 2010

All rights reserved. No part of this book may be reproduced or transmitted in any form or by any means, electronic or mechanical, including photocopying, recording, or by any information storage and retrieval system without the prior permission of the publisher and/or author.

www.Lulu.com
Lulu Enterprises, Inc.

ISBN: 978-0-557-42874-8

Celebrating the Mass

Contents

1

The Gathering

Ellis

If you forgive others their transgressions, your heavenly Father will forgive you. But if you do not forgive others, neither will your Father forgive your transgressions.
Matthew 6:14-15

The Mass is supposed to be a celebration, so one would think that the opening would be grand and celebratory. That is not the case, however, for we begin the Mass with our heads hung low, conscious of our sinfulness and begging God's forgiveness. My most memorable personal encounter with forgiveness involved a boss I once had named Ellis.

I spent my childhood in Catholic New Orleans, surrounded by priests whom I admired and by neighborhood idols who were going off to the seminary to study for the priesthood. One of these idols was my older brother. So naturally, when I finished eighth grade I went off to St. Joseph Seminary, a minor seminary across Lake Pontchartrain north of New Orleans. I studied there for six years, spending all my teenage years studying religion, meditating, and keeping myself free of contamination by the world. This was, after all, a Benedictine monastery, and the time was before the Second Vatican Council. From there I went to Notre Dame Seminary in New Orleans, where I studied philosophy and theology for three years. In the summer after my ninth year as a seminarian I worked in an inner city parish in New Orleans, and the direct vision of the difficulty of priestly life scared me. I came home to Mobile and told my parents that I was not returning to the seminary. I made the right decision, and I have never second-guessed it, but at the time it was a traumatic experience. I felt like a failure, and it was hard for my family not to treat me like a failure. After all, nine years had gone for naught, or at least so it seemed.

For the next eight years I did useful things – two years teaching English in the Yucatan, three years in the army, three years teaching sixth grade – but without any direction to my life. Dolores changed all that, and a year after we were married we set out for California so I could pursue an academic career. I studied Russian at the Monterey

Institute of Foreign Studies for two years, and did so well that I was given a fellowship to pursue PhD studies at the University of Illinois in Champagne-Urbana. It wasn't long before I had established myself as a leading student in the Slavic department at Illinois, president of the honor society, publications in scholarly journals, invitations to review books for journals, to speak at an international conference in Montreal, to teach a summer course at the Catholic University of Lublin in Poland. I studied night and day for six months prior to my PhD exams, but I went into them somewhat cocky, because I was on top of the world. Until, that is, they informed me that I had failed. I will never forget that evening, walking into our apartment and crying on Dolores' shoulder like I have never cried before or since.

I could have taken the exams again six months later, but for a variety of reasons I did not. I loaded up my family and came home. Because I spoke Spanish I landed a job in the export business in Thibodeaux, Louisiana, and in 1975 I was invited to join an export company in Mobile, where my family had lived since 1947. The man who hired me had just become president of the company, and I was the first new person he brought into his young administration. Ellis and I hit it off well, and I started moving up fast. In just a few short years I moved up into management, my salary nearly tripled, and I was becoming known in the field. I traveled all over the world for the company, to Australia and Germany, to Mexico and Russia, to Jamaica and New Zealand, to Denmark and the Dominican Republic. One Monday morning in the eighth years of my work with that company, Ellis came in my office and told me that because of the shortage of business I was being terminated.

I sat around the house for two months moping. I could not help but think of my nine years in the seminary, of my six years studying Russian, and now of these ten years in the export business, and I kept thinking of myself as a triple failure. During months of angry loneliness, I searched the Scriptures for thoughts from God about forgiveness; I received the January 9, 1984 issue of Time magazine, with Pope John Paul II and his attempted assassin on the cover and the headline: "Why Forgive?"; I reflected on Pope Paul VI's address at the opening of the second session of the Council, in which he looked at the non-

Catholic observers he had invited there and asked for forgiveness from all those who feel themselves to have been injured by the Catholic Church; I heard the story of a priest of our diocese who preached the homily at the funeral of his murdered brother and publicly forgave the murderer. It was during this turmoil that I received the invitation to give a talk at a local parish on the subject of forgiveness. I knew that that there was no way I could stand before that group and talk about forgiveness as long as I was unable to forgive Ellis, the man who had been the instrument of so much hurt in my life. So I began to focus all my efforts on the healing process of forgiveness.

Pope John XXIII inspired me with what he said in his encyclical *Peace on Earth*: "One must never confuse error and the person who errs.... The person who errs is always and above all a human being, and in every case he retains his dignity as a human person. He must always be regarded and treated in accordance with that lofty dignity." So to help me make that distinction between my former boss and whatever he did to hurt me, I wrote a prayer asking God to bless this man and take care of him. I carried the prayer around with me and prayed it from time to time. This practice worked wonders, and a great amount of healing took place in saying that prayer. Martin Luther King also inspired me when he wrote in his book, *Strength to Love*, that "the forgiving act must always be initiated by the person who has been wronged, the victim of some great hurt."

With my prayer I had taken the first step. But now I had to take the next step, and this I did about a month before I spoke at the parish. On a weekday morning I collected my thoughts, said a quiet prayer for strength, and dialed the familiar company number that I had not used in ten months. The receptionist and I chatted for a moment and then she switched me to Ellis. He was so happy to hear from me, he asked how I was doing, he asked about Dolores and the children. I asked how he was doing, and how things were going at the company. It was as unremarkable a conversation as you can imagine, but in the course of carrying it out I was relieved of a year's burden of hurt. I never actually said "I forgive you," but he could tell that it was good between us again. His voice smiled at me. My voice smiled back with the happiness that comes from being free. We ended up arranging to have lunch about a week later.

When we come together at Mass, the first thing that we have on our minds is mercy and forgiveness. We confess our own sinfulness, reflecting on questions such as these: What condition is my life in? Am I a loving, caring person? What condition is my home in? Are things in order there? Is the environment peaceful? What condition is the world in as we approach the table? Are we at peace with each other, or are we fighting wars, abusing spouses and children, marginalizing the poor, killing children, executing criminals, terrorizing innocent people, torturing terrorists? Are we one human family, or are we separated from each other by race, economic status, religion, political preference, or sexual orientation? What prompts us to approach God asking for mercy?

I often think of Ellis as I join with the other worshipers in asking for God's mercy. Lord, have mercy on us for all our offenses against you. We claim to worship only you, the one true God, and yet how often we bow down before the altars of pride and selfishness, power and possessions, prestige and pleasure. Christ, have mercy on us for all our offenses against our brothers and sisters in the human family. We claim to accept your commandment to love one another, and even to love our enemies, and yet how often we abuse, alienate, oppress, neglect, and even kill each other. Lord, have mercy on us for all our offenses against ourselves. We claim to respect ourselves as part of your wonderful creation, and yet how often we misuse and abuse our bodies, waste our abilities, and ignore our most basic needs.

May almighty God have mercy on us, forgive us our sins, and bring us to everlasting life.

2
The Proclamation of the Word
Raymond

All scripture is inspired by God and is useful for teaching, for refutation, for correction, and for training in righteousness...
2 Timothy 3:16

Once we have gathered for Mass, we spend some time listening as the Word of God is proclaimed. Sacred scripture is the very foundation of our faith, and we listen to it every time we gather for a liturgical celebration. The scriptures convey a powerful message of divine love and redemption, and for that reason we rely on scripture scholars to help us understand that message. I once had a moving encounter with one such scholar.

After my ten years in the business world, I spent one year unemployed, memorizing all the want ads in the local paper, working at a couple of part-time jobs, and going through most of our savings. I was rescued by a friend who told me of an opening in the religion department of the local Catholic high school. I applied for the job and was hired to teach scripture to ninth graders and social justice to twelfth graders.

I felt ready to teach scripture, but I did not like the textbook because it talked about the Bible but did not involve the students in reading the actual text of scripture. I wanted my students to be comfortable reading the Bible on their own, so I began preparing handouts for them based on our reading of specific texts in the Bible. I chose texts that were important for understanding the history of God's people, such as the call of Abraham and Moses with the brining bush. I chose stories that adolescents could relate to, such as David and Goliath and the finding of Jesus in the Temple. For a couple of years I produced more and more of those handouts, which were eventually collected into two textbooks which were published in my fifth year of teaching in the high school and were used by the school for about ten years.

It was around that time that the Office of Religious Education sponsored a lecture by the biblical scholar, Father Raymond Brown. Brown was Sulpician priest in the diocese of Baltimore, Maryland who taught for 23 years at the Protestant

Union Theological Seminary in New York. He was widely regarded as a preeminent biblical scholar, the author of some forty books and the recipient of 24 honorary doctoral degrees by universities all over the world. He was president of the Catholic Biblical Association, the Society of Biblical Literature and the Society of New Testament Studies, and was appointed to the Pontifical Biblical Commission in 1972 by Pope Paul VI and again in 1996 by Pope John Paul II.

The talk took place on a Saturday morning and the hall was packed. Father Brown spoke for about an hour and a half, and he spoke the whole time about scripture. I had come to his talk prepared to be educated and edified. What I had not come prepared for was to be moved to tears by the holiness of this great scholar. The last part of his talk was like a blur to me because I was so overwhelmed by the force of his personal sanctity, and I could hardly focus on what he was saying.

When the talk ended, there was a reception in the hall to give people the opportunity to visit with each other and to say a few words with Father Brown. During that reception the director of the Office of Religious Education and asked me if I had time to go to lunch with her and Father Brown. She was taking him to the airport after the talk, and they would stop on the way and have lunch. Of course, I accepted the invitation, and a half hour later I was sitting in a restaurant booth opposite Father Raymond Brown, with no one else present but Sister Maureen. I felt extremely honored to be there and I did not want to make a fool of myself, so I allowed Father Brown and Sister Maureen to control the conversation. And what did Father Brown want to talk about? He wanted to talk about my experience in teaching scripture to high school ninth-graders. What aproach was I using? What was the students' reaction to scripture? What were my major obstacles? How did I handle this or that aspect of scripture? A world-class scholar spent an hour with me, and spoke the whole time about me and my experience teaching scripture.

It took me a while after I got home to connect the holiness that Raymond Brown exhibited in his lecture with the holiness that he exhibited in that restaurant conversation. Sanctity consists in selfless love for others. I would not be surprised Raymond Brown, that great biblical scholar, was particularly drawn to what Paul wrote in his letter to the Philippians: "Do nothing out of selfishness or out of vainglory; rather, humbly regard others as more important than yourselves, each looking out not for his own interests, but everyone for those of others" (2: 3-4).

Look out for the interests of others: that is the message of the scriptural passages that are proclaimed to us at Mass after we have finished declaring our individual and communal sinfulness. Sunday after Sunday the message comes through, a message of right relationships with others through justice and peace. We hear in the first readings things like Isaiah speaking of God's servant establishing justice on the earth, or Paul expressing his wish that you may be found rich in the harvest of justice. We meditate, using psalms like Psalm 72 singing the praise of the ruler who has pity on the lowly and the poor. Then in the Gospels we hear things like Jesus condemning those who see him hungry and do not give him food, or the parable of the rich man who will be kept out of paradise because he ignored the sufferings of the poor man at the gate of his home.

The liturgical year presents us with a rich collection of biblical texts which focus our attention on the injustices found in our sinful world and God's challenge to us to work for a better world. In the years following the publication of the bishops' pastoral letter on the economy in 1986, I prepared reflections on the Sunday liturgies and sent them out to all the priests of our diocese. Those reflections were published in the mid-1990s by Sheed & Ward under the title *To Love and Serve.* I found, for example, that just in the Ordinary Time of Year A, I was prompted by Scripture to reflect on the destruction of God's creation, the attacks on human life and dignity, contempt for the poor, the isolation of the homeless, militarism and the death penalty, but also to respond to the challenge to seek justice, to make ours a society in which people do not go hungry, to end the cycle of violence, to live lives of service to our brothers and sisters in need, to find God among the little people, the sick and dying, the poor and hungry.

God's word to us, proclaimed at every Mass, is a message of reconciliation not just between us and God but also among all

God's children. It teaches us to put the well-being of others ahead of our own selfish interests. Raymond Brown understood that.

3
The Homily
Hugh

Rolling up the scroll, he handed it back to the attendant and sat down, and the eyes of all in the synagogue looked intently at him.
Luke 6:20

When we read the scriptures privately, the Spirit can touch our hearts and affect the way we live our lives. We often miss things, however, either because of our shortsightedness or because of our inability to understand the text, our ignorance of the context in which the text was written. Scholars like Raymond Brown can lead us into a deeper understanding of that context, but their interest is primarily academic, and that is not what is required in the liturgy. The proclamation of the Word in the liturgy calls for a pastor, a shepherd, someone who can guide us from the readings at Mass to their application in our lives. The homily is a pastorally guided reflection on the readings intended to help us leave Mass better prepared to work for the coming of the kingdom.

Let me tell you the story of Hugh and his unforgettable homily.

I spent my four years of high school and my first two years of college at the Benedictine monastery across Lake Pontchartrain from New Orleans. At that time – the 1950s – there were about thirty or forty priests, some of them running the seminary, some running the monastery, and some working in nearby parishes.

The celebration of Masses followed the pre-Vatican II format. On weekdays there was a Mass at the main altar for all the monks and seminarians, while at about a dozen side altars individual priests were saying their private Masses with individual servers. On Sunday there was a "High Mass," which was a sung Mass with priest, deacon, and subdeacon. The monks took turns preaching the homily at this Sunday High Mass, and since there were so many priests in the monastery, a priest might have only one or two opportunities a year to preach.

This particular Sunday, it was the turn of Father Hugh, a tall, thin, fair-skinned, and very nervous man who was my literature teacher. I liked Father Hugh because he was kind and gentle and did not yell and scream at me when I did not read the literature assignment (which was most of the time). I was happy to see that it was Father Hugh who rose this Sunday to preach to us. He walked up the stairs to the pulpit which straddled one of the broad pillars of the church, and we looked at him with anticipation. He had brought no book or notes with him, so that meant that he would speak to us, not read to us, and we liked that. Father Hugh looked back at us, and then he looked down, as though he were trying to gather his thoughts. The seconds began to add up, and we squirmed in our seats as Father Hugh stared silently into space. It became clear to us that Father Hugh's mind had gone blank, and after about the longest three minutes imaginable, Father Hugh made the Sign of the Cross, descended from the pulpit, and returned to his seat.

I have never forgotten that moment, and I think of it especially when I am forced to listen to a half-hour sermon that bores me to death. I also think of that moment as a statement on scripture, for maybe Father Hugh was on to something. When all is said and done, what can we possibly add to scripture? God has said it all, and if we would but listen, all the noise of unbelief and oppression and war would be silenced. Perhaps Father Hugh preached the best homily possible, reminding us that God will have the final word, and that silence is the proper human response to the majesty of God and God's Word. "Be still and confess that I am God!" (Ps 46:10).

Of course, Father Hugh preached wonderful homilies on other occasions, and I have heard my share of good homilies by caring, thinking pastors. The homily, I have learned, helps prevent misunderstandings of the biblical text. To those of us who are inclined to read the biblical message in individualistic terms – me and God – the homily helps us grasp the communal approach of scripture – us and God. When we are tempted to live pampered lives in splendid isolation – and what we do, after all, is no one else's business – the homily suggests an alternative lifestyle, one based on self-giving for the sake of others.

The homily shows us how scripture can help us understand what is taking place in our world, not in the way that some would have it, as though the bible is filled with prophecies of contemporary events, but rather as illuminating the forces of good and evil that struggle in every age for the mastery of the world. We fight our wars with different weapons today, but the forces that drive to us kill each other are the same ones described in scripture: the struggle for power and the will to dominate, disregard for the humanity of others, the desire for increased possessions, and class warfare. The "different" people in our society are no longer the Hittites or the Samaritans, but we discriminate using the same tools of oppression described in scripture: pride, selfishness, disregard for the humanity of others, clannishness, and the will to power. We find ever new ways to torture the land, but the challenge to respect God's creation remains as valid today as it was in biblical times, and the obstacles to that respect are the same as ever: pride, greed, and disregard for God's handiwork. The homily helps me understand all that.

The homily helps us appreciate the Old Testament on its own terms. The way our lectionary is ordered, primacy is given to Gospel texts, so that the texts from the Old Testament are chosen on the basis of their correspondence with a theme found in the Gospel text. This could leave us with the impression that the Old Testament has no value apart from its connection to the Gospels, but the homily provides a corrective to that impression. Philip A. Cunningham, a professor at Boston College and a leading figure in Jewish-Christian dialogue, has published lectionary introductions[1] which help us recognize the beauty of the message of the Jewish scriptures apart from any connection to the Gospels.

The homily helps us deal with problematic New Testament texts. There are New Testament texts about slaves obeying their masters and wives obeying their husbands, about women not speaking in the assembly, about the Jews being responsible for the killing of Jesus. These passages cannot just be read and

---

[1] Philip A. Cunningham, *Proclaiming Shalom: Lectionary Introductions to Foster the Catholic and Jewish Relationship*, Collegeville, MN: Liturgical Press, 1995

ignored. They must be tackled, and the homily gives us the opportunity to identify the human elements in scripture so that the divine message can shine brilliantly.

The homily allows us to identify the challenge of the Bible so that we can accept it as befits God's people. Blessed are the poor in spirit, scripture teaches, and we reflect in the homily on how the world sets up the rich in first place while Jesus put the poor on top of the world. Blessed are they who mourn, scripture teaches, and we reflect in the homily on how the world tells us to seek happiness at all cost while Jesus saw happiness in mourning. Blessed are the meek, scripture teaches, and we reflect in the homily on how the world values power over others while Jesus praised the meek. Blessed are they who hunger and thirst for righteousness, scripture teaches, and we reflect in the homily on how the world encourages self-fulfillment while Jesus told us to work for justice. Blessed are the merciful, scripture teaches, and we reflect in the homily on how the world says that the merciless succeed while Jesus proclaimed blessed the merciful. Blessed are the clean of heart, scripture teaches, and we reflect in the homily on how the world announces: Go for the gold! while Jesus taught us to keep our hearts pure. Blessed are the peacemakers, scripture teaches, and we reflect in the homily on how the world honors the winners of wars while Jesus celebrated peacemakers. Blessed are they who are persecuted for the sake of righteousness, scripture teaches, and we reflect in the homily on how the world sees the persecuted as losers while Jesus declared them the winners.

The homily allows us the opportunity to reflect on the connection between the two parts of the Mass, the liturgy of the Word and the liturgy of the Eucharist. In line with Jesus' challenge to be doers as well as hearers of the Word, we reflect in the homily on how we can learn from scripture the lessons we need in order to give ourselves up for others the way Jesus offered up his life for the world.

4

The Profession of Faith

Andy

Then the boy's father cried out, "I do believe, help my unbelief!"
Mark 9:24

After listening to the proclamation of the Word and after reflecting on it in the homily, we profess our faith, our belief in the Trinitarian God, in who that God is and in what that God has done for us. It is a faith that was a gift to me in my childhood and which I nearly lost as an adult. By now the reader has been introduced to much of my biography, so the story of my life which follows will contain some repetition. The difference is that I would like now to tell my life story from a faith perspective. This is the story of my faith life.

I was raised in New Orleans during World War II. We lived in a old, established neighborhood which was overwhelmingly Catholic and which breathed with the life of St. Ann parish, where we all attended school. My brother entered the seminary after the eighth grade, and my plan from my earliest childhood was to go to the seminary. We moved to Mobile after my fifth grade, but I never wavered in my plan to study in the seminary affiliated with the archdiocese of New Orleans. In 1950 I entered ninth grade in St. Joseph Seminary in Saint Benedict, Louisiana and did all of my high school at St. Bens as well as my first two years of college. After graduating from there I moved to Notre Dame Seminary in New Orleans, where I studied two years of philosophy and one year of theology. During the summer after my third year at Notre Dame, I got a summer job working at a Black parish in New Orleans, and within a few weeks I had decided that I did not, after all, want to be a priest. I let everyone know that I was leaving the seminary, but I had no intention of becoming less of a Catholic. I did not know what I would do, for I had never considered any other job but that of a priest, and I did not even know where to look for a new direction to my life. One day I was reading the New Orleans diocesan newspaper and came across an article inviting volunteers to teach in a boys'

Catholic middle school in Merida, Yucatan, Mexico. I went to New Orleans for an interview, and soon thereafter I was on a plane to Merida, having volunteered for two years as a lay missionary helping a Maryknoll priest who had just opened the Colegio Central in Merida. I spent two years there, teaching English and religion, and I would have returned for a third year had not the Berlin Wall just been built. I received a draft notice and decided to join the Army in the hopes that I would qualify for the Army Language School. During boot camp at Fort Jackson, South Carolina, we were given a battery of tests that would determine the kind of work we would do while in the army. The foreign language test would be my ticket to learning a new language, so I was anxious to do well in it. The test contained sixty questions, and the passing grade was 18. I made a 59, and they allowed me to choose any language I wished. I chose Polish because I had long been fascinated by the history of Catholic Poland. I spent the year 1962 in Monterey, California, studying Polish, and graduated with a grade of 98, the highest grade ever achieved up to that point.

My assignment was to a base in Bavaria, and on the nine-day voyage across the Atlantic, I was asked by the Protestant chaplain if I would conduct daily prayer services for the Catholics on board. During my time in Germany, I taught catechism to the Catholic youngsters on base, I spent a number of weekends at a Benedictine monastery, and I spent ten days in Rome, absorbing the atmosphere of the place which lies at the center of my church.

After leaving the army, I taught sixth grade at Our Lady of Lourdes School in Mobile, and during that time I met Dolores through a priest friend who had been in the seminary with me. Dolores was working at the Catholic School Office, and our wedding at St. Joan of Arc Church was attended by a number of priests. The following year we moved to Monterey so I could pursue Russian studies, and I supported the family with several part-time jobs, including helping the Oratorian Fathers to open a counseling center and teaching Latin in the local Catholic high school. I studied Russian two years in Monterey and made straight A's. In the Spring of 1969 I applied to the University of Illinois and was awarded a four-year fellowship.

The transition from the tiny Monterey Institute of Foreign Studies to the huge University of Illinois at Urbana-Champaign was difficult, but I eventually settled in and became a top student. I spent the summer of 1970 in Poland, teaching English to some of the faculty of the Catholic University of Lublin, and that experience resulted in the publication of several papers, invitations to review books for scholarly journals, and even to make a presentation at a scholarly convention in Montreal. I went to Illinois with the same strong faith that I had maintained since my childhood, but something happened in Illinois. I found myself growing distant from God and feeling confident in my own ability. The grade of 59 in boot camp, and the 98 in the Polish course, and the straight A's in Monterey studying Russian, and now the high grades at Illinois along with all the publications – all this went to my head, and I no longer felt any need to waste time fooling around with God. Time was precious for this ambitious student, and an hour studying a Russian novel was much more useful than an hour in church. So I stopped going.

By the Spring of 1972 I had completed the coursework for a doctorate, so I made plans to take the comprehensive exam in the Fall. I drew up a detailed schedule which had me studying all day every day for six months, taking breaks only for eating, sleeping, and on Thursday afternoons, a little time with the family. By the time of the exam I was exhausted but confident. The exam was a week-long ordeal, followed by a couple of weeks of anxious waiting while the panel of professors evaluated it. Their brief note informing me of my failure devastated me, and I recall being very angry at God, from whom I had sought no help. When we moved back to Mobile, I had no faith in God or in myself. Had it not been for Dolores, I am sure I would have despaired.

I could not find any work in Mobile and ended up working for a small company in Thibodeaux, Louisiana, which manufactured sugar cane equipment. They hired me because I spoke Spanish. Dolores tried to get me to go to church, and I did agree to go one Sunday. The priest, unfortunately, made a big spectacle of stopping in the middle of Mass and fussing at some teenagers, and I told Dolores not to bug me any more about going to Mass. After two years in Thibodeaux, I was hired by an export firm in Mobile, and we rented a house in one of the older neighborhoods of Mobile. By now we had three children, and I became uncomfortable with the Sunday morning situation, with Dolores going to Mass and me sitting at home reading the paper. I agreed to try Mass in Mobile, and it was not bad except for the horrible sermons preached by the elderly pastor. I started going to Mass with Dolores and the boys, but during the sermon I would slip out the side door with our youngest son, and when I heard the creed being recited, I went back inside and attended the rest of Mass.

It was not an ideal situation, but it worked. Listening to the readings every Sunday and participating in the Mass week after week, I gradually experienced somewhat of a revival of my faith. When we bought our own home in 1977 and moved into a new parish, I was not anywhere near where I had been earlier in my faith, but there was a spark. Somehow I got volunteered into teaching kids on Sunday mornings, and it was Andy and those other fourth and fifth graders who gave me back my faith.

That whole story lingers in the back of my mind every time I join in the profession of faith at Mass, because it is a faith that I very nearly lost. It is with joy now that I profess my belief in one God, a God who is not ours as opposed to theirs but rather is the God of Christians and Jews and Muslims and of all those who believe in God and all those who do not believe. I profess my belief in God the Father of us all, Father of the rich and the poor, Father of the young and the old, Father of the oppressed and their oppressors. I profess my belief in God the Almighty, the God of justice who, in the words of Mary, has shown might with his arm, dispersing the arrogant, throwing down the rulers and sending the rich away empty (Luke 1:51-53). I profess my belief in God who is maker of heaven and earth, of all that we can see for ourselves and all that is too hidden or too small or too far away for us to see, the maker of the earth that sustains and refreshes us in so many ways and that nevertheless we trample upon and lay waste to. I profess my belief in one Lord, Jesus

Christ, the only Son of God, eternally begotten of the Father, God from God, Light from Light, true God from true God, begotten, not made, one in Being with the Father. Through him all things were made. For our sake he came down from heaven to rescue us from ourselves. By the power of the Holy Spirit, he was born of the Virgin Mary, and joined the human race as one of us, sharing with us our struggles to mature, our physical and psychological sufferings, our tormented days and sleepless nights. I profess my belief that he was crucified under Pontius Pilate, he suffered, died and was buried for our sake, completing a life that was totally given to uplifting the lowly, freeing the oppressed, welcoming the outcast, preaching good news to the poor, identifying the narrow path that leads to salvation, and condemning religious hypocrisy. I profess my belief that he rose on the third day, confounding all those who deal in death, who fight wars, perpetrate genocide, abuse children, marginalize the poor, neglect the elderly, oppress the handicapped and the alien. I profess my belief that he ascended into heaven, leaving to us the task of completing the work he began of bringing people together, spreading love where I live and work, ending all forms of killing, providing for everyone's needs, and helping everyone to know God and to live as God's children. I profess my belief that he will come again in glory, to judge the living and the dead, to settle accounts with the killers of innocent people, the declarers of wars, the perpetrators of genocide, the abusers of women and children, the oppressors of those who are different, and the bystanders who witness injustice and do nothing. I profess my belief that once it comes, his kingdom will have no end, for there will be no return to the old ways of death and destruction. I profess my belief in the Holy Spirit, the Lord, the giver of life, and we worship and glorify that Spirit of life together with the Father and the Son. I profess my belief that the Spirit has spoken through the Prophets, telling us to make justice our aim, to listen to the voice of the poor, and to care for the orphan and widow. I profess my belief in one holy catholic, and apostolic Church, the community of disciples of Jesus who are gathered in his name as a sacrament of universal salvation, a sign that God cares for everyone and offers hope and love to all who will accept it. I profess my belief in one baptism for the forgiveness of sins, and I reject as contrary to the will of God all division within the community of baptized believers. I profess my belief in the resurrection of the dead, after which there will be no more killing or being killed, and my belief in the life of the world to come, when all sorrow will be banished and there will be pure joy.

This is our faith, a gift from God that I appreciate now more than ever and that I nurture and guard every time I celebrate Mass.

5
The Prayers of the Faithful
Ivan and Jose

Do not worry about anything, but in everything by prayer and supplication with thanksgiving let your requests be made known to God.
Philippians 4:6

At the point at which the Liturgy of the Word meets the Liturgy of the Eucharist, we present our petitions before God, basing them on the condition in which we find ourselves. Two incidents in my life have helped me understand the Prayers of the Faithful.

The first took place in Moscow in 1978, when the Cold War raged and Brezhnev was chairman of the Communist Party. I was working for an export company, and we had decided to have a booth at an international equipment display. Our sales representative from Germany would be there, and I would join him as a Russian interpreter. The exhibit lasted over two weeks, and I had many interesting encounters during that time, but the most interesting involved a man whom I shall call Ivan.

I was standing in front of our booth, watching the occasional passers-by on this slow day. A man walked slowly up to me, leaning lightly on his cane. He spoke a hesitating but correct English with an obvious but not too heavy Russian accent. Throughout our conversation he wore a half smile and the darks of his eyes moved left and right in sharp jerks.

“Is it not difficult to live in a country in which there are so many Negroes?” he asked. “Yes, it is a problem,” I answered, “for both blacks and whites, but it is not a problem altogether bad for us or one that we cannot live with.” “I can’t believe that,” he said. “I am sure that if you had the chance to live in a country without Negroes, you would take it.” The last thing I wanted was a race argument, so I proceeded cautiously but politely. “Other countries may not have blacks but they have enough problems of their own.” He smiled somewhat sarcastically and fixed his jerking eyes on me. “Yes,” he said, “other countries have their problems. We have ours, you know.” I looked at him motionless.

“I am sure you have seen our problems,” he continued, after a pause. I remained quiet. “Tell me,” he said, “what do you see on the faces of our Soviet people? Do you see faces that are happy or unhappy?” I had to say something, but I also had to be careful, since there was no way of knowing who this stranger was. “I don’t think I have been here long enough to answer that question,” I replied. “Well, I will tell you what you see. You see neither happy nor unhappy faces. What you see are the faces of people that do not think, for if we ever thought about our condition we could not stand it.” For a brief moment we stood with our eyes fixed on each other. He said some other things, but I did not hear them or at least do not recall them.

Our Christian faith and tradition challenges us to think about our condition, for it is only in reflecting on where we are and where we are headed that we can make the kind of change in direction that Jesus spoke of in his charge to his followers to “Repent, and believe in the gospel” (Mark 1:15).

The other story took place in the Caribbean in May 1982, and it involves a man whom I shall call Jose. The company sent me on a trip to visit our contacts in Puerto Rico, the Dominican Republic, and Jamaica. The stop in Puerto Rico was completed, and I boarded the plane for the flight to Santo Domingo. We took off in beautiful clear weather, but halfway between Puerto Rico and Dominican Republic, the weather got very nasty. By the time we were approaching the airport in Santo Domingo, the tropical rainstorm was extremely heavy. We passed over the runway and I remember thinking that we seemed too high to land and too low to circle around. But circle around we did, and by the time the plane touched down, we had already passed up more than half of the runway. The pilot slammed on the brakes, but it was not enough to stop the plane by the end of the runway, and we went barreling into a field of low-lying trees. The plane was bouncing rather violently, and things were flying around the fuselage. It was seconds rather than minutes before the plane finally stopped and settled into the rain-soaked field, but in those seconds the man in the seat next to me must have screamed out at least ten times: “Jesus, help me!” What startled me was that in those same few seconds, I remember thinking that it was too late to start approaching Jesus for help, that by now Jesus knew very well if I was truly interested in his help.

I will not comment on the theology underlying our two reactions to the possible tragedy that faced us. I do think, however, that in a sense we were both right: we do need to seek God's help, and we need to do it not just in times of desperation but rather on a regular basis. This is what we do in the Prayers of the Faithful: we seek God's help in handling the circumstances in which we find ourselves.

We reflect on the condition of our Church, and we ask God to bless its leaders and to keep the church faithful to its scripture and to its long tradition of caring for the poor and the stranger.

We reflect on the condition of our country, and we ask God to bless its leaders and to help us build a tradition of respect for human rights and justice for all.

We reflect on the condition of our parish, and we ask God to bless its leaders and to help all those in our parish who are suffering and in need.

We reflect on the condition of our homes, and we ask God to bless us so that our homes will be filled with love and mutual nurturing.

We reflect on the condition of society, and we ask God to help us eradicate poverty, eliminate homelessness, provide care for the suffering, end discrimination, and prevent wars.

We reflect on the condition of our lives, and we ask God to help us overcome all those things which are holding us back from entering the kingdom.

6
The Presentation of Gifts
Marja

Therefore, if you bring your gift to the altar, and there recall that your brother has anything against you, leave your gift there at the altar, go first and be reconciled with your brother, and then come and offer your gift.
Matthew 5:23-24

We begin the Liturgy of the Eucharist with the presentation of gifts. The primary gift, of course, is Jesus Christ, who will be offered on the altar to his Father, but we are invited to unite ourselves to that gift, to present our lives as offerings to God. A major experience in my life has helped me understand that call, an experience that involves the cross and a person named Marja.

The cross is the Christian symbol par excellence. We begin most prayer sessions with the Sign of the Cross. We carry the cross at the head of our processions, and we place the cross in the most prominent places in our churches, both inside and outside. For centuries Christians built their churches in the shape of a cross. Priests bless with a cross, and bishops wear the cross on their breasts. Individual Catholics wear crucifixes around their necks, and they places crucifixes on the walls of their homes. Walk into any Catholic institution and you will find a crucifix hanging somewhere, and very likely in every room. All over the world the remains of Christians lie buried under crosses.

The cross is for Christians a symbol of redemption. We venerate the cross on Good Friday, and during evening prayer of Holy Week we sing: "Hail, O Cross, our only hope." The *Catechism of the Catholic Church* quotes St. Rose of Lima: "Apart from the cross there is no other ladder by which we may get to heaven."

I spent the month of July 2000 studying the Holocaust at Yad Vashem in Jerusalem. My studies and subsequent research made me painfully aware of another perspective on the cross: Jews see the cross as a sign of hate and condemnation. Robert McAfee Brown tells the story of the mother of a Jewish friend of his on the faculty of Stanford University. Entering the Stanford Memorial Church, she commented, "Every time I see a cross I tremble. What is for Christians a symbol of God's love of them, is for me a symbol of their hatred of us."[2] What else is a Jew supposed to think? The persecution of the Jewish minority began after the Roman emperor Constantine had a vision of a cross and the writing: "In this sign you will conquer." Christian persecution of Jews began in earnest during the Middle Ages with the Crusades, those military actions against so-called unbelievers that took their name from the cross. And when it came time for the "final solution" of the "Jewish problem," the symbol chosen was a swastika, the figure of a disguised cross that had been used in the Christian catacombs of Rome. The Polish Jew, Stanislaw Krajewski, insists that "the legacy of history is clear: for centuries the presence of crosses indicated the power of the Church. It also signified a discrimination of Jews."[3]

I did not realize the impact my new awareness of the dark side of the cross was having on me until the next Good Friday. Standing in line, waiting to kiss the just-unveiled cross, I suddenly cringed. How could I possibly kiss this symbol so often (mis)used to persecute others. I kissed the cross, of course, as I had done all my life, but it was not easy.

I returned home and began a process of reflection on the cross, beginning with its symbolism. The Christian cross takes the shape of a tree, and we make the connection between that tree and the tree of life mentioned in Genesis 3:22. The cross is life-giving, and therein lies the shame associated with all the killings that have taken place in the crusades and at other times under the banner of the cross. Believers in the cross, those who aspire to "take up their cross and follow Jesus," should be the first to protect life, and what a difference it would have made if European Christians had fought en masse in defense of Jewish life. Maybe then Jews would have developed some respect for our theology of the cross.

The Christian cross also takes the form of the human figure standing with arms outstretched, a symbol of the human race for

---

[2] Robert McAfee Brown, "The Coming of Messiah: From Divergence to Convergence?" in Michael D. Ryan, ed., *Human Responses to the Holocaust: Perpetrators and Victims, Bystanders and Resisters*, New York: Edwin Mellen Press, 1981, p. 206

[3] Stanislaw Krajewski, "Auschwitz at the Threshold of the New Millennium," in John K. Roth and Elisabeth Maxwell, eds., *Remembering for the Future: The Holocaust in an Age of Genocide*, 3 vols., Houndmills, UK and New York: Palgrave, 2001, vol. 3, p. 334

which Christians believe Jesus was offering his life. Implied in this symbolism is the unity of the human family and a repudiation of all those actions and attitudes which fracture that unity. Believers in the cross, those who aspire to "take up the cross and follow Jesus," should be the first to defend the unity of the human family. The history of Christian anti-Judaism and antisemitism represents a denial of the true meaning of the cross, and it is no wonder that that Jewish woman trembles every time she sees a cross.

The most important aspect of crucifixion theology, however, is not the symbolism of the shape of the cross but the attitude and action of the one crucified. The Gospels make it clear that Jesus voluntarily gave up his life, that he saw the solution to whatever the problem was not in the death of his enemies but in his own sacrifice. Those who appeal to the cross as their banner should see in it a sign of giving one's life for others, not taking another's life or allowing another's life to be taken. When Martin Luther King told his followers that if any blood should flow in the struggle for civil rights, it should be Negro blood, he was being faithful to the Christian theology of the cross. When leaders of the churches made decisions during the Holocaust not to endanger Christian lives by protesting too loudly against the taking of Jewish lives, they were being unfaithful to their own theology of the cross.

With all this positive theology of the cross, we must also consider the possibility that the cross has in some ways been counter-productive, and Peter Gilbert's assertion must be taken seriously: "The German death camps are a stark and jolting declaration that the Cross by its infliction of suffering did not overcome suffering. Indeed, perhaps the reverse is true; by a process of abstraction it has made Christians insensitive to suffering, and enabled the ghastly inhumanity of the Holocaust to become reality."[4]

My reflection on the cross left me with many questions. How can we make credible our appeal to the efficacy of the cross, and the image of sacrificial, voluntary suffering it presents? How can

---

[4] Peter Gilbert, "Theological Impact of the Holocaust," *Christian Attitudes on Jews and Judaism*, No. 58 (February 1978), p. 11

the image of the cross be embodied, and not just proclaimed, in the life of the Christian community? Will the cross survive in a form that is credible to people of good will of whatever faith tradition, or will it survive in a form that forces Christians into hypocritical stances? How can we come across as less threatening to Jews and still maintain a central symbol that is a symbol of execution?

Mary Boys, who has been very active in the Jewish-Christian dialogue, has grappled with the issue of the cross.[5] She recognizes that "this central symbol of Christian life has a shadow side," and there is a need to "redeem" the cross and relearn its true symbolism. She admits that at one point "I was prepared to argue for its replacement or at least for lessening of the importance of the symbol of the cross in Christian life," but after a moving liturgical experience she decided to recommend instead that Christians "repent of its abuse in order to reclaim its power."

Like Mary Boys, I struggled to regain my affection for the cross, but I was meeting with little success. Then one day it happened unexpectedly. I was reading the book by Mordecai Paldiel, *The Path of the Righteous*, about Christian rescuers of Jews during the Holocaust. Paldiel tells the story of a Polish Catholic named Marja Maciarz, whose daughter-in-law had agreed to care for a Jewish boy but became scared and decided to turn the boy in to the Gestapo. Marja took the boy from her daughter-in-law and cared for him till the end of the war, and when the parents came for him—they had miraculously survived Auschwitz—they found their son being lovingly cared for by Marja. The couple decided to leave Poland to start a new life elsewhere, and they turned a family house over to Marja. The couple signed the deed, but when it came Marja's turn to sign, they discovered that she was illiterate: she signed the deed with a simple cross. I was profoundly touched by this story because I have always revered the cross as a symbol of love and self-sacrifice, and Marja Maciarz embodied that symbolism: not the emperors who fought in the name of the cross; not the crusaders who had crosses emblazoned on their shields; not the inquisitors who held up the cross as they burned Jews at the stake; not the Catholic

[5] Mary C. Boys, "The Cross As a Christian Symbol," *Has God Only One Blessing: Judaism as a Source of Christian Self-Understanding*, Mahwah, NJ: Paulist Press, 2000, pp. 223-244

perpetrators, collaborators, and bystanders who closed their doors during the Holocaust and began their prayers with the sign of the cross; not the prelates who, crosses lying on their breasts, refused to speak out on behalf of their Jewish brothers and sisters; not the cross placed at Auschwitz in an attempt to hijack the Holocaust from the Jews; but the signature of Marja Maciarz, the simple, illiterate woman of faith who risked everything to save a little Jewish boy. In *that* cross I could believe.

The next Good Friday, I bowed down before the cross of Marja Maciarz, and I kissed it with joy, faith, and a renewed commitment to give my life for others.

After we have listened to the proclamation of the Word during Mass, we bring our offering to the altar. Marja offered herself, her very life, which she put on the line in order to save the little Jewish boy, and her example leads me to reflect on what I have to offer. What can I give to my relatives and friends, to my parish, to my city and state and country, to the world? What talents can I offer to a world that needs my help? What wealth can I offer to the 1.3 billion people who live on less than a dollar a day? What power can I share with the powerless? What love can I offer the forgotten? The church encourages us to bring our gifts to the altar because she knows that we have much to offer.

To our relatives and friends we can offer love, support, and a commitment to serve them in every way possible.

To the poor of the world we can offer not just a share of our wealth but more importantly, our active concern for their plight and our commitment to work for the structural changes that will lessen the burden of poverty.

To the people of our parish we can offer prayerful concern, participation in the programs of the parish, and a share of our personal and financial resources for the benefit of everyone in the parish.

To the victims of war we can offer relief from their sufferings as well as our dedication to ending the curse of militarism and the divisions that cause wars.

To our children and to all the children of the world we can offer our love, our support for their education, and our resolve to fight against the physical, psychological, and sexual abuse of children.

To the sick and dying we can offer comfort, respect for their dignity, active concern for them in their time of need, and support for universal health care.

To the universal church we can offer prayers, concern for the well-being of believers everywhere, and interest in what takes place in other parts of the church.

To prisoners we can offer prayers, time – if that is possible, and commitment to the creation of a criminal justice system that promotes restoration rather than revenge.

To the people who live in our town, city, or region, we can offer support for the economic, social, and political well-being of the entire community.

To the elderly we can offer love, active concern for their needs, and support for the kinds of policies and programs which make it possible for the elderly to live in dignity and respect.

To the rich and powerful we can offer concern for their spiritual well-being and cooperation in working for a more just and equitable society.

To women and men we can offer dedication to the creation of a society in which all people are given equal respect and everyone, regardless of gender, can contribute their talents to society and benefit from its advances.

To minorities we can offer support for their having a voice in society and for those policies and programs that protect their rights.

To the unborn we can offer support for everything that helps their mothers be healthy and loving and everything that will make it possible for them to be born into an infancy that will not end prematurely and suffer from deprivation.

These and many other gifts we can bring to the altar at Mass, always keeping in mind what Maria Maciarz understood, that our greatest gift is our very lives.

7

The Great Prayer

Hank

The Lord Jesus, on the night he was handed over, took bread, and, after he had given thanks, broke it and said, "This is my body that is for you."
1 Corinthians 11:23-24

The Mass is first and foremost a memorialization of the Last Supper, the meal that Jesus ate with his disciples on the night before he died. All the accounts of the meal report that Jesus took bread, said the blessing, and broke it (Matthew 26:26; Mark 14:22; Luke 22:19; 1 Corinthians 11:23-24). After the resurrection it was in the breaking of the bread that the two disciples in Emmaus recognized the risen Lord (Luke 24:35). The gospel of John makes it clear that Jesus' body was not broken (19:33), so the brokenness is not physical but existential. What Jesus was acting out was the brokenness of our lives, and every time I think of that, I think of Hank.

My first visit with death row inmates at Holman Prison in Atmore, Alabama, was on the occasion of a gathering of members and supporters of Project Hope to End the Death Penalty. Project Hope was an organization begun by some of the inmates, and while the board of directors consisted of six inmates, membership in the organization was open to anyone. The warden allowed the members to meet on occasion, and I was invited to one of these gatherings.

The meeting took place in a large central room surrounded by a hallway, with glass walls separating the room from the hallway. About fifteen death row inmates, along with about thirty or forty "outsiders," were present at the gathering, which lasted from ten in the morning to two in the afternoon. There was a formal meeting, which consisted of opening and closing prayers, introductions of key persons, speeches by some inmates and outsiders, and discussion of organization business. The meeting was followed by lunch, which consisted of sandwiches and drinks purchased from vending machines in the room – we were not allowed to bring food, or anything else, for that matter, into the room. Each table had at least one inmate sitting at it, and the inmate who sat at my table was Gary Brown. For the rest of the time spent in that room, we mingled with the inmates and chatted with the outsiders. The drive home to Mobile took an hour, and the thought occurred to me as I was driving that I was surprised at how normal the inmates seemed. Then I felt bad for having this thought because it meant that I had been successfully conditioned to regard death row inmates as some kind of subhuman monsters.

Jesse, a cofounder of Project Hope and chair of the board, invited me to visit him, and I accepted his invitation. He had to request that my name be placed on his list of approved visitors, and that took some time, but eventually we got together. Family and friend visitations took place on a given Saturday of each month, so I went on that Saturday, received approval from the guards to enter, emptied my pockets, was searched, and then was escorted into the meeting room along with all the other relatives and friends. The inmates came in after a few minutes, and we had four hours to spend with them. I sat at a table with Jesse and was told not to speak with any of the other inmates. We discussed organization business and life on death row, and for lunch we had sandwiches and drinks from the vending machines. I told Jesse that I had enjoyed meeting Gary Brown and that I would like to come back to spend a day with Gary some time.

A couple of months later I was informed that Gary had succeeded in having my name placed on his list of approved visitors, so I arranged to spend the next visiting Saturday with him. Gary and I spoke about the organization and what I could do to help it, and he talked in general terms about his situation on death row, expressing the hope that his appeals might be successful. We never talked directly about the crime that resulted in his being on death row, but the last time I saw Gary he gave me a paper he had written about his life, including his crime and his conversion to Jesus. The paper went into great detail about Gary's growing dependence on drugs and his frequent encounters with the law. When it came time to speak of his capital crime, Gary says in his paper: "Well, a couple of months later, these guys that I knew and I got drunk and planned to go out and rob this homosexual that we knew. We did this, but in the process, things went sour and the homosexual was killed. I was arrested a few days later and charged with capital murder." This is how the *Birmingham News* described what happened: "Brown and the other men went to McGraw's home on Memorial Day to drink with him with the plan that he would pass out and they could rob his home. But McGraw said he had to work the next day and couldn't party with them. The men then attacked him outside his trailer and dragged him back inside. Brown struck the first blows, and repeatedly stabbed McGraw with a pocketknife as Bankhead stood over him with a skillet. McGraw was stabbed in the back 59 times, his throat and neck were slashed 16 times and his face showed three knife wounds. After the slaying, the trio loaded some of his household appliances into their car and took $67. Neighborhood children found his body." [*Birmingham News*, April 25, 2003, the day after Gary's execution by lethal injection.]

Gary and I had a very pleasant visit, and we decided that it would be good for me to spend time with other members of the board of Project Hope. It took us a while to arrange, but eventually I returned to Holman Prison, this time with my son, Matthew. Matt spent the four hours with Gary, and I spent the time with Henry Hays.

Hank's story is one of the most notorious to come out of Mobile. In 1981 a Black teen, Michael Donald, was on his way to a service station to get a pack of cigarettes when he was abducted by two Klansmen and driven to a remote area in Baldwin County, across the bay from Mobile. Henry Hays and James "Tiger" Knowles Jr. beat Donald unconscious with a tree limb, and then they took his body back to Mobile where they slipped a rope around his neck, strangled him, and hanged his body from a tree. Hays slashed Donald's throat three times to make sure he was dead. Prosecutors said Hays and Knowles had driven around Mobile "looking for a Black man to hang" because they were angry that an interracial jury had failed to convict another Black man for killing a White police officer in Birmingham. The Klansmen selected Donald at random and lynched him to show Klan strength and scare Blacks from serving on juries. Hank would end up being electrocuted on June 6, 1997.

Hank and I had a pleasant meeting, and Matt enjoyed his visit with Gary. I helped them make plans for the forthcoming Project Hope gathering, which took place shortly thereafter. This gathering was a different experience for me because by now I was known to more of the members and I was helping the inmates in several different ways, such as printing and distributing their newsletter. Once again, there were about fifteen inmates present and about forty outsiders. Halfway through the meeting, I was asked if I would agree to meet separately with the board members, and I said yes. Inmates kept coming up to me and informing me of the status of the negotiations with the warden. Just before two o'clock, they told me that the warden had agreed, and that when all the other outsiders left, I was to remain in the room. At two o'clock the room was emptied, and for about ten minutes I sat by myself in absolute silence. I heard a noise and looked up to see one of the inmates enter the hallway, and I watched as they removed the handcuffs and the chains that tied his legs together at the ankle. The inmate entered, and the same process was repeated for each of the other five. Finally we were all together, and they closed the glass door. The six inmates, including Jesse, Gary, and Hank, sat in a circle with me, and the first thing we did was join hands and pray. We then spent an hour discussing the business of Project Hope, and they were interested in talking about me and my family. They focused on my teaching of social justice to high school students, and they wanted to learn from me what the students were saying about the death penalty and how I approached the subject in teaching the class. We talked and smiled and even joked a bit, and it was a very pleasant conversation. These six death row inmates, four of whom were Black, seemed to get along well together. They cared about each other and about inmate population in general, and the meeting was filled with references to "the Lord."

At the end of the meeting we stood up, held hands, prayed, and then hugged each other. It was an unforgettable moment watching Hank, the convicted Klansman, hug the four Black inmates. Some years later I told this story to one of my classes at Spring Hill College, and a Black female student objected very strongly to my positive presentation of Hank at that meeting. It turned out that she was Michael Donald's cousin, and in her view Henry Hays did not deserve any kind of respect at all. I told her that I understood her anguish and hurt, but that I was simply telling her what I saw: Hank was accepted by four Black men as their partner on the board, and Hank hugged all four of them, acknowledging them as his brothers.

On the night before his own execution by crucifixion, Jesus, gathered with the disciples, "broke the bread" and gave it to them. Brokenness is at the center of the execution of Jesus and its memorialization in the Mass. It was broken humanity that hung on the cross, and it is broken humanity that Jesus offers his Father on the altar: those whose bodies are broken through old age and disease, through war and violence, through self-abuse and accidents, and those whose lives are broken through separation and divorce, through unemployment and homelessness, through alcohol and drug abuse. It is not just people like Gary and Hank whose lives are broken; it is all of us who are broken, one way or another. That is why we gather around the altar, not to point our fingers at others but to acknowledge our own need for redemption, our own brokenness.

At Mass we also share the cup, which Jesus said to do in memory of him. It is a cup of blood, memorializing the blood shed on the cross but also connecting us with the blood that is being shed by opposing armies, by murderers and indiscriminate killers, by governments that kill their own citizens, by abusing parents and spouses.

The Great Prayer of the Mass, the memorialization of the death of Jesus on the cross, is a celebration of the presence of God. God is present, not in the presidents and generals who perpetrate wars but in the sufferings of the young men and women and innocent civilians who die in wars. God is present, not in those who execute others but in those who are executed, as Jesus was. God is present, not in the oppressors but in the broken lives of the oppressed.

I experienced the presence of God in that circle of death row inmates, whose lives had been broken and whose blood would eventually be shed by the state in which I live. I experienced the presence of God in watching Hank hug those four Black men. I experience the presence of God in every Mass.

8

The Our Father

Walter

Our Father in heaven, hallowed be your name...
Matthew 6:9

As with all the other sacraments, we begin the reception of the Eucharist with the recitation of the Lord's Prayer, the prayer to our Father in heaven that Jesus taught us. My first experience with fatherhood involved Walter, and I would like to tell you his story.

Walter was born in 1905 in New Orleans, the oldest of seven children. He never finished elementary school, and instead went to work to help support the family. He ended up working for the telephone company, and was expert in sending Morse Code. In 1928 he met a young school teacher at a King Cake party, and he and Eulalie LeBlanc were married on July 9, 1930. They would have five children in their first six years of marriage, two more during World War II, and two more after the war. They lived in New Orleans, moved to Mobile in 1935, returned to New Orleans in 1940, and moved back to Mobile in 1947. Walter worked for the telephone company in New Orleans until his father asked him to join his gasoline distribution company in 1945. For two years he worked in Mobile while his family lived in New Orleans, and he would come in every other weekend. His family moved to Mobile in 1947, and in March 1949 Walter took over the operation of a gas station that had been operated by his brother, who was killed in an automobile accident. He ran the station for five years, and then in 1954 he exchanged the station for four stations in counties north of Mobile. He started adding new stations in other towns, and at the height of his business, he had 14 stations in such towns as Butler, Grove Hill, McIntosh, Purdue Hill, Yarbo, Leroy, Deer Park, and Pine Hill in Alabama, and Leakesville and Lucedale in Mississippi. His business flourished until the gas shortages of the early seventies took their toll, and then blindness gradually handicapped Walter during the course of the eighties. Nevertheless, he held on to the business in ever diminishing form until quite late in his life.

Walter was a self-educated man and always impressed people with his knowledge and understanding of things. He was a true southern gentleman, which meant that he carried with him the baggage of southern prejudices, and yet it is to his great credit that he did not raise his children in an atmosphere of prejudice. He had a great sense of humor and loved to play practical jokes. He and his wife had an interesting relationship that mellowed in their later years, and in the end their 65 years of marriage were a beautiful sign of love to all who knew them.

At the time of his death Walter had 9 children, 46 grandchildren, 68 great-grand-children, and 16 great-great-grandchildren. I was the fourth of his children. My dad was not very expressive of his feelings, and I do not have any affectionate memories of my childhood. I never remember him hugging me in my youth or kissing me or telling me that he loved me. I also have no negative memories of him beating or abusing me, and I do remember taking walks with him to City Park. What happened to my dad was that he lived to be almost 99, and old age combined with blindness brought on a softening of his personality. In the last ten or fifteen years of his life, he told me he loved me so many times that it more than made up for all the previous decades. I always knew that daddy loved me, and now I had his words to support it.

We have a wonderful Father in heaven who loves us more than we can ever know. Jesus wanted us to love our Father in heaven, and he directed us to pray to him. And so we pray.

We reflect on our Father in heaven, who loves all his children unconditionally. We reflect on the ways in which his name is honored, through peacemaking and concern for the poor and protection of the environment, and also on the ways in which his name is dishonored through pride and selfishness. We reflect on the ways in which the Father's will is done on earth, by loving relatives and caring friends, by communities that work at resolving differences peacefully, by people organized to make changes in a world filled with injustices, by religious groups of all kinds who link their worship of God with their work for a more just society.

Then, for the third time at Mass, we present petitions before God. We ask the Father to give us the things we need every day: food for our hungry stomachs, drink for our thirsty tongues, love for our empty hearts, hope for our longing spirits, wisdom for our probing minds. We ask him to forgive us for all we have do to ourselves, to our relatives and friends, to all those with whom we work and worship, and to all those whose lives are affected by our actions, decisions, choices, public attitudes, votes, as well as by our inaction. For our own part, we forgive those who have offended us in any way by their actions, decisions, choices, public attitudes, votes, as well as by their inaction. We ask the Father to help us to stay on the straight and narrow path, and save us from the power of evil.

Walter did the best he could in being a father to me. He brought me closer to my Father in heaven, and I love him for that.

9

The Communion Service

Jim

The bread of God is that which comes down from heaven and gives life to the world.
John 6:33

The Mass is a meal, so food and drink will be provided, just as food and drink were provided in the garden of Eden, and food and drink were provided in the Sinai desert, and food and drink were provided in the land flowing with milk and honey, and food and drink were provided for the thousands who came to hear Jesus teach. The Mass is a meal, and in eating that meal I often think of my meal with Jim.

The American bishops spent several years producing their pastoral letter, "Economic Justice for All," in November 1986. A conference on the forthcoming pastoral was held in June of that year at Fordham University in New York. Its purpose was to enable educators to begin communicating to the larger community the concepts of the bishops' letter. Participants came from all over the country, from California to New York, from Nova Scotia to Alabama. I attended as a member of the Archdiocesan Peace and Justice Commission and as a religion teacher at McGill-Toolen High School. I accompanied Sister Carole Gurdak of the Catholic Schools Office.

None of the talks or workshops were devoted to the actual text of the pastoral letter, as it was assumed that everyone knew its contents. One talk took a key concept of the letter, the option for the poor, and showed what it means and does not mean, its link to Scripture and the social teaching tradition of the Church, and its practical implications on the social and personal levels. Another speaker showed how the pastoral represented a shift in perception through its application to the U.S. economy of the Biblical concepts of creation, covenant, and community.

There was some broad criticism of the letter. One speaker pointed out that the pastoral is a message from us (the Church) to them (the actors on the economic stage); it would have been better, he said, if the approach of Pope John Paul II in *On Human Labor* had been used, starting off with work (in which we all participate) and building toward a system of justice for all. Another speaker criticized the pastoral for focusing on the U.S. economy, which, he said, no longer exists: there is only a world economy now.

But there was universal praise for the pastoral as a major event in the American Church's perception of the Gospel's implications for the economy. As one speaker pointed out, American Catholics in the 19th and 20th centuries had to be superpatriots in order to overcome Protestant reservations about them. But now that American Catholics have become an economic force to be reckoned with, the pastoral letter challenges them to become countercultural, in a sense, in order to aid in what it calls the unfinished business of the American dream of liberty and justice for all.

A high point in the conference for me came in a speech that called for a bonding between bishops, priests, religious, and lay people. The pastoral would go nowhere if we would not all work together. Especially important are the ordinary laity, who are the primary agents in the economy and without whose involvement the pastoral would become the property of the intellectuals, an irrelevant piece to be stored in our libraries.

The conference was organized and run by five women religious, and most of the participants were nuns. Those same five sisters had conducted a conference three years earlier on the bishops' peace pastoral. For that conference they aimed at 300 participants, and got 320. This time they aimed again at 300 participants, and got 160. This was going to be a harder pastoral to implement, for everyone felt threatened by nuclear war; while not everyone perceived the threat of an unjust economy.

Of the 160 participants, only two – Sister Carole and I – came from the region south of Virginia. I was proud of my diocese and saddened by the lack of interest shown by a part of the country where there is at least as much economic injustice as elsewhere.

The most beautiful and meaningful Eucharists have always been the ones in which I do not receive Christ as much as I give myself to him. When, at the closing liturgy of the conference, I sang the communion hymn, "Here I am, Lord," I experienced that giving of self and I knew that something special was happening in my life.

As soon as Mass was over, I asked a friend if she would go outside and take my picture with Sister Carole. We all went out and walked to a corner sign reading 'Fordham University,' which was the backdrop I wanted for my picture. We found there one of the conference speakers, Sr. Clare Fitzgerald, waiting to catch a taxi to LaGuardia. We also found Jim, a street person whom my friend began speaking with. We took a couple of pictures, and as we were going back in to get our belongings and leave, I learned that Jim was told to wait because our friend was coming back to get some food for him. He had told her he wasn't doing too well because he hadn't eaten in a long time. I asked my friend if I could take him with me instead, and she said yes.

"Come on, Jim," I said, "come and have lunch with me." "Where's my little girl?" he asked.

"I'm taking her place," I answered. "Do you mind?" "No," he said, "but I would like to take my son with me." "Go get him," I replied. "I'll wait."

I waited about five minutes. Jim disappeared across the street and returned alone. He looked disturbed. "He's gone," Jim told me. "He's pouting about something."

We started off. Jim never asked me where we were going. He simply put his hand on my shoulder and walked beside me. I will never forget that hand on my shoulder. It was so heavy, like dead weight, as though he didn't have the strength to hold it up alone.

I lead him towards McDonalds, about six blocks away. I started asking about his son, and eventually learned the following about Jim. Originally from Florida, he came to New York, married a Puerto Rican woman, and they had four children. The family was split by his drinking problem. She lives in Puerto Rico with two of the children. Jim has been living in the streets for eight months with his youngest son, a semi-retarded 19-year old. Nothing was said about the fourth child.

Jim's head was bent down. He had to make a great effort to straighten his neck when he wanted to look at me. The only other noticeable physical feature was a huge sore on the back of his right hand, which he said he got from the grates he slept on.

Looking at the lowered head and the hand wound, I could not help but think of the crucified Jesus.

McDonalds was nearly filled. We walked up to the line, and I asked Jim if a hamburger would be okay. "With everything on it," he answered, "lettuce, tomato, everything." I wanted to sit with Jim as an equal, so I made a point of ordering the same meal for both of us: their largest hamburger, fries, and coke. We found a table in the middle of a row of tables for two. As soon as we sat down the person next to us got up and left. Gradually all the others in the row left, and no one sat in those places the rest of the time we were there. It was a very obvious isolation, and I felt different, out of place. I remembered the point made by Sr. Clare in her talk, that Christianity is the alternative lifestyle and that Christians, if they are true to their calling, have to stand apart from the normal way of doing things.

Jim and I started eating. I took one bite of my hamburger, and Jim had finished a third of his. I took a second bite, and Jim had nearly finished his hamburger. While I was chewing my third little bite, Jim finished devouring his hamburger and started on the fries, which he stuffed in his mouth seven or eight at a time. Before I knew it, Jim had nothing left but the ice in his coke, and he was chewing away at that. I was halfway through my hamburger and had not touched my fries or coke. I poured my fries in his container and told him to eat them.

"I'm sorry," he said, "it's just that I haven't eaten in a long time." I told him not to worry. That was his first defense of his dignity.

"I don't eat a lot," he said. "I get fat too easily. This here is going to take care of me for two days. 1 mean, this is solid food, I won't have to eat for a couple of days."

"There's one thing 1 don't understand," Jim said, while he was waiting for me to finish eating. "The Bible says that God's children have to suffer, and so we suffer. Now don't get me wrong, 1 can take it. I've been shot and cut up," and as he said this he lifted up his shirt to reveal a horrible scar the length of his torso. (The wound in the side of Jesus, I thought.) "1 can take the suffering," he continued, "but why, maybe you can tell me, why do God's children have to suffer? Do you know why?"

"No, Jim," 1 said, "1 don't know why."

"I don't either, and I really don't understand why little children have to suffer. You know what I would do if I had a million dollars?" he asked. "I would give every bit of it to retarded children. I mean, I can handle the suffering, but it's hard on children." No self-pity here; Jim felt bad for those less fortunate than him.

We cleaned off our table and went out. It was time to part. Jim lifted his head, thanked me, and threw his arms around me in a warm embrace. Then he asked if I would give him something for his son. I gave him some money, and something inside me made me say that I hoped the money really went for food for his son. "I'm no liar," Jim responded. That was his second defense of his dignity.

"God bless you," he told me. "He already has," I replied. "He let me have lunch with you." Jim smiled for the first time and threw his arms around me again. Then we went our separate ways.

In their pastoral letter the bishops spoke about solidarity with the poor. I resolved that I would not eat for the rest of the day: I wanted to be hungry with Jim.

During the conference one of the speakers told of the need to put a name on the poor. He pointed out that the only time Jesus gives a parable character a name is in the parable of the rich man and Lazarus. It's not enough to know that x number of people go hungry every day; we have to recognize the poor as individuals, we have to give a name to the poor person. I now know his name. It's Jim. I have seen, touched, heard, and smelt the poor, and his name is Jim.

There was another "Jim" long ago who wrote a letter we hold to be inspired by God. He wrote: "If a brother or sister has nothing to wear and no food for the day, and you say to them, 'Good-bye and good luck! Keep warm and well fed,' but do not meet their bodily needs, what good is that?" (James 2:15-16) The bishops called on us to ask that question anew in 1986. Even more, they called on us, not to absolve Jim of all responsibility for his situation, but to review the social attitudes and structures that kept him and his son in the streets.

The culmination of the Mass is the communion service, in which we eat the sacred bread and drink the sacred wine. It is an opportunity to express solidarity with the suffering people of the world, not in a superficial way but in the most fundamental way of becoming one with the other. The body of Christ – Jesus unites me in the depths of my being with his body and with all those whose bodies are broken through old age and disease, through war and violence, through self-abuse and accidents. The blood of Christ – Jesus unites me in the depths of my being with his blood and with all those whose blood is being shed by opposing armies, by murderers and indiscriminate killers, by governments that kill their own citizens, by abusing parents and spouses.

It is at the communion service at which the Mass becomes a meal, and hunger is satisfied. My communion with Jim involved a meal, and most human interactions involve the satisfaction of some kind of hunger. In 1975 the American bishops issued a document which reminded us of the different hungers experienced by people. People hunger for God, not a petty god who blesses one country and not another but a magnificent God who loves everyone passionately and favors the poor and the outcast because they are so unfavored by others. People hunger for food. About 800 million people in the world are so hungry all the time that they cannot lead active and healthy lives. Pope John XXIII said that we all share responsibility for the fact that populations are undernourished. People hunger for freedom and justice. They don't want to be oppressed. They don't want to be stereotyped and discriminated against. They don't want to be relegated to the margins of society. People hunger for the Spirit. They want life and love. They want to be included in the action, and they want to be filled with good things. They don't want to be alienated and powerless. People hunger for the truth. They don't want to be misled by self-serving political interests, by greedy corporate interests, by self-righteous religious interests. They hunger for the truth, for an end to the lies they are being told about why we have to fight wars and why there have to be people who are poor and hungry and homeless. People hunger for understanding. Christians and Muslims don't understand each other, Democrats and Republicans don't understand each other, pro-life and pro-choice people don't understand each other, the rich and the poor don't understand each other, teenagers and the rest of the world don't understand each other. People hunger for understanding, so that they can glory in the richness of the diversity of the human race. People hunger for peace. After a century in which over one hundred million people were killed in wars, most of them civilians, people want peace in the world. The problem is: Where to start? Pope John XXIII gave us the answer: There can be no peace among people, he said, unless there is peace within each person. People hunger for Jesus. They long for the truly human that we experience in Jesus. They long for the life and love of God that we experience in Jesus. They long for the richness of Jesus' teachings about the way people ought to live together. They hunger for Jesus, not the Jesus that some have created, a Jesus who takes sides in wars, and justifies power-grabbing, and condemns all who are not like them, but the Jesus we encounter at Mass, a Jesus who gives his entire life for others, a Jesus who welcomes the rich and the poor to the table, a Jesus who feeds the hungry and focuses our attention on the suffering people of the world.

Jim and I shared our hunger for food and for love. It was a blessed meal.

10

The Dismissal

David

He sent them to proclaim the kingdom of God and to heal.
Luke 9:2

The Mass ends with a blessing and a charge to go out and serve God in the world. The implication is that we are to go out as changed people, renewing the face of the earth. We are to be witnesses to God, and through us others are to come to know God. Unfortunately, our actions sometimes turn others away from God, and that is what happened to David.

I spent the month of July 2000 in Jerusalem studying the Holocaust at Yad Vashem, the Israeli institute for Holocaust studies. I was sent there by McGill-Toolen Catholic High School and Mobile Jewish Welfare Fund, with a scholarship from Yad Vashem arranged through the National Catholic Center for Holocaust Education at Seton Hill University.

The course was made up of lectures by some of the most renowned Holocaust scholars in the world: Jeremy Cohen (Church Antisemitism in Daily Life During the Middle Ages), Zvi Bachrach (The Rise of Modern Antisemitism), David Bankier (Nazi Racist Ideology, Nazi Policy—Persecution of the Jews, The Final Solution), Yehuda Bauer (Jewish Leadership—Youth Movements, Jewish Leadership—The Judenrat), David Silberklang (Operation Reinhard: The Murder of Polish Jewry, Response of the Allies), Gemma Del Duca, S.C. (The Vatican and the Shoah—Post Holocaust Christian Theology), Pesach Schindler (Jewish Faith during the Holocaust), Ziva Amishai-Meisals (Holocaust and Art). Mixed in with these lectures were some field trips: a full day trip to the Diaspora Museum in Tel-Aviv, an overnight tour of the Jordan Valley, Belvoir Crusader Castle, Ein Gev, Golan Heights, Golan Winery, Ghetto Fighter's Kibbutz, and a visit to Massada and the Dead Sea.

Sprinkled through all these lectures and field trips were testimonies by survivors of the Holocaust. Ruth Brand was taken away from her home in Romania at the age of 13. She experienced transportation in a cattle car, the horrors of Auschwitz and Bergen-Belzen, and the loss of her entire family. Yona Laks and her late sister Hannah were among the twins who endured the infamous Mengele experiments. Pola Susswein described for us the years she spent in the concentration camp of Plaszow near Krakow. Lucy Mandelshtam of Vienna told us about her separation. when she was 18 years old, from her mother and sister, both of whom were killed by the Nazi Germans. Hanna Rojanski of Krakow described her experiences at Auschwitz. We heard testimony from Dov Freiberg, a survivor from the escape from the death camp at Sobibor. We even met with two survivors who were on Oskar Schindler's list, and they gave their testimony standing at Schindler's grave.

The most moving testimony for me was given by David Brin. David described for us his experiences in the Lodz ghetto. He was only eleven years old when he saw his parents and siblings for the last time, and is the only surviving member of his entire family. David finished his story, and then he talked about its effect on him. I don't believe in God, he said. After what I saw and experienced as a young boy, I am convinced that there is no God. If there were a God, he said, he would have to be a monster to allow such things to happen, and a God-monster is an impossibility. So there is no God.

David spoke this very calmly, but it had a profound effect on me. I had become very interested during the course on the role of ordinary Christians and the role of the institutional church in the Holocaust. I knew that at the time of the Holocaust, the vast majority of the people in Europe were baptized Christians. I knew that many of the perpetrators had been raised Catholic, including Hitler and Goebbels. I knew that many of the collaborators and bystanders were practicing Catholics. The Holocaust was not a Christian event, but it was carried out with the help of people who were attending, or had attended, Mass. We have no way of knowing what scale it was on, but there can be no doubt that practicing Christians, including practicing Catholics, participated in the isolation, persecution, torture, abuse, and killing of Jews during the Holocaust.

The events that take place during the Mass – the experience of God's forgiveness, the proclamation of God's Word, the offering of ourselves in union with Jesus Christ, the memorialization of the death of Jesus, the sharing of Jesus' body and blood – none of these have meaning if we leave the assembly unchanged, as though nothing had happened. So important is the dismissal that we customarily refer to the service in terms of the dismissal: we call it the Mass, from the Latin *missa*, the sending forth. The charge that is given at the end of Mass – Go in peace to love and serve the Lord – sounds like a polite farewell, but is in the form of a command. There is work to be done, and it must be done in a spirit of peace, love, and service. Perhaps David would believe in God today if enough Catholics at the time of the Holocaust had accepted the challenge at the end of Mass.

Go in peace to love and serve the Lord, to turn your homes into places of joy and unconditional love.

Go in peace to love and serve the Lord, to help all humanity come together as one family, with no artificial separations and with no one excluded.

Go in peace to love and serve the Lord, to work for an end to wars and all forms of violence.

Go in peace to love and serve the Lord, to give your life for others.

Go in peace to love and serve the Lord, and know that you go with the blessing of your church.

www.ingramcontent.com/pod-product-compliance
Ingram Content Group UK Ltd.
Pitfield, Milton Keynes, MK11 3LW, UK
UKHW041834200726
13854UKWH00003BA/1126

9 780557 428748